MOVING FORWARD TO BRIGHTER DAYS

SHERRY LEONARD

WESTBOW
PRESS®
A DIVISION OF THOMAS NELSON
& ZONDERVAN

WestBow Press books may be ordered through booksellers or by contacting:

WestBow Press
A Division of Thomas Nelson & Zondervan
1663 Liberty Drive
Bloomington, IN 47403
www.westbowpress.com
1 (866) 928-1240

Scriptures are taken from the King James Version of the Bible.

ISBN: 978-1-5127-8186-1 (sc)
ISBN: 978-1-5127-8185-4 (e)

Library of Congress Control Number: 2017904690

Print information available on the last page.

WestBow Press rev. date: 4/11/2017

CONTENTS

A special thanks to my sister Michele,
Brothers Bernard, and John (deceased 2015)

Moving forward to brighter days is dedicated to my family,
to allow everyone to know that the storms of life do not last
always, continue to move forward, and the brighter days will
come. Moving forward to brighter days is created to uplift,
encourage, edify and to bring hope to people around the world.

ALPHA AND OMEGA

I am Alpha and Omega, the beginning and the end,
I am Alpha and Omega, your very best friend,
I am Alpha and Omega, the first and the last,
I am Alpha and Omega, I know your present,
future and past.

TRUE BEAUTY

True beauty dwells within. It is not about the color of the skin,
It is not an issue of black or white,
true beauty reflects in the day and night.
What is on the inside will show up on the outside.
Don't allow the makeup, fake hair, or sculptured nails,
or colored eye contacts fool you.
Yes, it is nice, but is your flesh only a mess?
Is it only being dressed up, what is really within?
Do not allow the great physic (body shape), false teeth,
or flashy clothes cause you to be blind; guard your mind
and remember that true beauty begins within.
so check the heart, is it real? Look deep inside, what do you
feel and what do you see? True beauty starts within.

PRICELESS

You are worth much more than rubies and gold,
you are valuable and can't be sold.
You are more than a house, more than a car,
more than a diamond ring, or a famous movie star.
You are worth so much.
Man, can't offer what God has already purchased, he has paid the price.
The drug dealers, pushers, and pimps, they are only wimps.
Do not fall prey and do not sell out.
Don't sell yourself for things. You are priceless.
Yes, material things are nice, but wait
You are precious, more than a meal, more than a vacation trip,
more than a piece of furniture, more than a designer purse, fur,
or fancy pair of boots, more than an expensive sports vehicle,
or immaculate house, you are priceless.
You are priceless from the dope house to the courthouse to God's house,
You are priceless,
from guilt and shame and lots of blame, you are priceless,
from molding, making, and lots of shaping, you are priceless,
from the pit to the palace, from a prostitute to prophetess,
from a pimp to a pastor,
from a homosexual to head of hospitality,
from the jail pit to the pulpit, you are priceless,
remember that you are priceless and can't be sold;
you are worth more than silver and gold,
When you know who you are, and to whom you belong,
you can't be bought and you can't
be sold, you are priceless and worth more than silver and gold.

THE COLOR OF LOVE

Is love black or white, red or blue, young or old, age four or ninety-two?
The color of love,
Is love pastel, deep purple, or sky blue, is love old or is love new?

The word of God says in (KJV):

> Leviticus 149:18 Thou shalt not avenge, nor bear any grudge against the children of thy people, but thou shalt love thy neighbor as thyself: I am the Lord

> (KJV) Proverbs 17:17 A friend loveth at all times, and a brother is born for adversity

> (KJV) Matthew 5:44 But I say unto you, Love your enemies, bless them that Curse you, do good to them that hat you, and pray for them which despitefully use you, and persecute you;

and that true love cast out fear, but what is the color of love?
Is it clear, shiny, bright, or dull; or is it like a rainbow,
with multi-colors, standing tall? Is it striped, polka dot, plain, or plaid?
Is love happy or is love sad? What is the color of love?
We are taught to love, to care, to give, to share,
but what is the color of love?
Is it beige; is it brown, yellow, or orange?
Look around, what do you see?
Images of Christ Jesus are what it should be. This is the color of love.

LIFE IS A JOURNEY

Life is a journey that everyone must go through, but the road that you choose, is what is important to you. The road goes in all directions, so ask the Lord for his protection. There is wide road with many things to do, just do not become a fool. The narrow way is straight and can lead you to the Pearly gates. On your journey, the road of life takes you on mountains and sometimes in the valley low, and sometimes you may do some things and journey in a way that only you and God may know. Life is a journey, and while on your journey, you may grow, or you may lose your soul. The journey can carry you to heaven or to the grave, so be strong, fast as well as pray, and each day, journey in a new way. Expand your mind, spread your wings, journey through life and do the right things.

WHERE ARE OUR SONS?
(A prayer of protection for the one, who plants the seed to produce our sons)

Where are our sons – Is that our son with the big gun, who
shot the other guy just for fun? Is that our son, sitting in jail,
or is that our son, on the way to hell, on death row paying for a
crime, serving time, for a reason that he still does not know?
Is that our son, the one who has been lied on, fired, and
cannot get hired, so he is smoking a joint because he has
no point? Parents are confused, so he begins to use drugs,
and started hanging with thugs, where are our sons?
Are they roaming the streets, seeking after
every woman they can meet?
Are their pants pulled down to the ground? Are they sleeping in
lots of beds, wishing they were dead because they came in contact
with a deadly disease that breaks them down to their knees,
Where are our sons?
Our sons are hungry, and thirsty too, and we must
help them so they will not become blue.
Are our sons on a trolley or in an alley, or just hooked
up with Nancy, Tina, and Sally? Are they
The professor, the instructor, the conductor, the engineer, the pastor,
the father, or president, the drill sergeant, police officer or judge?
Your son, my son, uncle, dad, father, nephew or friend,
Where are our sons in the end?
No more little boys full of laughter and joy,
Where are sons?
Are they coming in late from their first date, only to find out his
name was Nate? Hey, are they gay, or have they just gone astray?
Where are our sons? Some strong, some never want to be wrong,
some meek, but not weak, where are our sons?
Good men, bad men, men, men, men,
where are our sons?

WHERE DID THE LITTLE GIRL'S GO?
(A reminder to pray, to protect and cover girls everywhere)

All of a sudden, they began to grow, where did the little girls go?
From the mother's breast, and the dad's chest, where did the little
girls go? from Sunday school to high school, which way did they
go? Did they go off to college to earn a degree, or did she decide
to stay home, and have many babies? Where did our girls go?
Did she go to work, or become a big flirt? Did she become an
entrepreneur? or end up scooping up cow manure? Did she go off to
jail or become the sister with her body for sale? Where did the girls go?
Did she lose her virginity when she was yet so sweet to a young boy,
that she had to meet? Little girl left home all alone, then the parents
get mad when something goes wrong. Where did the little girls go?
Did she turn to the bottle or to crack? Where are the little girls at?
Is she walking the street, chasing after every man she can meet?
Where did our little girls go? Is she dead or in your bed? Where did
the little girls go? They once played jump rope, and on the swings;
now they are doing some wild things; they used to sit out on the
porch, using their eyes as a wide scope; now they are chasing dope,
only to get tangled up with false hope. Where did our little girls go?
Did she hide or disappear where nobody knows; did she become the
preacher, the teacher, the well-known speaker, the representative?
Is she the senator, a top model, a judge, lawyer, airplane pilot,
customer service rep, a doctor, a nurse, or the woman driving the
hearse? Is she a mother or a cop undercover? Where did the little
girls go? Is she the singer, or the party girl swinger? Where did the
little girls go? Daddy's little girl, mommy's little star, somebody's
sister, niece, aunt or grandchild. your little girl, my little girl, with
the beautiful braids, pretty curls, bows, ponytails, and fairytales.
Is she the multi-million dollar star, or the woman sitting at the
bar? Is she the evangelist on Sunday morn', or is she the one
with the fake name doing porn? Is she the Christian who is born
again, or is it a saying to cover her sin? Where did the little girl's
go? All across the world from state-to-state, city-to-city, county-
county, country-to-country, where did the little girl's go?

STAGES OF LIFE

First a baby, then a toddler, in between, and next a teen, these are the stages, and phases of life, school, school, and more school, the stages and phases of life, your twenties, thirties, and then your forties, marriage, children and then they say over the hill, these are some stages and phases of life. Doing things on your own, only to realize that you did a lot of things wrong, this is called the stages and phases of life. Growing older, hopefully wiser, and getting gray hair, the stages, and phases of life. The ups and downs, good times and bad times too, these are all a part of the stages, and phases of life. The hustle, the bustle, the tears, the laughter, the joy, the pain, the stain, and the strain, all of these things is the stages and phases of life.

STRONGER

Stronger we are growing by his grace, stronger as we seek his face, stronger as the Shepherd leads, stronger as we are on our knees, although we cry, sometimes not even knowing the reason why, yet stronger, we are growing in the Lord.

Allow God to unfold your circumstances in life, don't hold on to any grudges or strife. Allow Jesus to direct your life and continue to grow In Christ.

SEASONS
(Dedicated to my friend Renee Owens)
Ecclesiastes Chapter 3

Seasons come, and seasons go,
the snow will come, and the wind will blow,
the sun will shine, the rivers will flow,
the stars will twinkle, and the moon will glow,
there will be peaks, and also the valley, mountains low,
and mountains high, summer breeze,
autumn weed and different colors of the leaves,
seasons do change,
April showers and the flowers blooming in May,
some things go, some things stay,
but I promise you, that the seasons will change.
There will be seasons of joy, and seasons of pain,
seasons of laughter, and seasons of sorrow,
you will be young, and you will grow, develop,
mature to become older,and wiser seasons will come,
and seasons will go.

FAMILY

John 15:5 I am the vine, ye are the branches: He that abideth in me,
and I in him, the same bringeth forth much fruit; for
without me you can do nothing.

John 15:16 Ye have not chosen me, but I have chosen you, and
Ordained you, that ye should go and bring forth fruit, and that your
fruit should remain: that whatsoever ye shall
ask of the Father in my name,
he may give it to you.

When you think of your family, what do you think?
When you look at the family, what do you see?
All types of fruit that come from the tree.
Family should be there when the world turns it's back,
there to help one another get back on track.
We don't have control of who our family members are,
we were not able to choose our parents – they created us.
Not every family, but this family is unique, not jealous or to
belittle anyone, but uplifting, supportive and encouraging. This
family is full of love to give, to share, not to condemn or compare.
This family is willing to go the extra steps, the extra yard, and for
some the extra mile, after mile, after mile to help one achieve and
that is because we believe. We are not perfect, and yes some have
gone astray, but we still embrace our family with love today.
We dwell in different cities, some in different states,
and some may be out of shape, some may be deceased,
but what they have deposited, yet it lives.

We come together to celebrate where it all began, with
mama and papa and God has been and still is the head of
man. So enjoy your family, your life, and your friends and
until we meet again, we are all some kind-of-kin.

F=Freedom
A=Altogether
M=Multitalented
I=Intellectual
L= Loving
Y=Yoked up
That is the Leonard, Thompson, Driskill, Morgan, Keys,
Kraft, Hodge, Daniel, Ford, Barnes, Lee, Brown, Marbury,
Lauderdale, and all the other names, and when you put them
all together, you have family that originated from the seed
that blossomed into a beautiful tree called FAMILY

MINISTRY

Ministry, the church, the saints, the aints and the minister
The Church is designed to help shape the family; the church building
is for the people to join and get on one accord; it is a place of healing;
not a place for chilling, it is the Godly hour not the social hour,
It is the place to feed the sheep, not a place for the sheep to fall asleep.

It is a place for healing, not hurting, rejecting or to hinder anyone,
It is a place to share your gifts, and talents, not to compare, compete
or to be jealous of anyone. It is a place of worship, adoration, and
praise, not a place of confusion or to cause anybody to go astray;
It is a place where love is spread, not gossip.
The Saint, and the Aint – Inside of the church building are the
saints and the aints, some are fake, and some just don't know
how to relate. Some are on time, simply while others straddle
in late. Some lights shine, some were never lit, but yet they
come to the House of God, week after week and just sit, and
sit, and sit. So little time, and so much to be done, but when
the pastor calls for a servant, do they serve or do they run?
Labors are few or should we narrow it down to two, so be your
own judge to see where you fit in, you're either one or the other a
saint or an aint. So when your time is up, and when you die, you
get the pie in the sky or you will be the empty shell going to hell.
The Minister – The Minister is there around the clock, his or her job
is never done, it just does not seem to stop. They must feed the sheep
more than one meal a week or else the sheep will be frail and very
weak. A shepherd takes great care of the sheep, so the sheep will not
wonder off into the dangerous streets. The minister delivers the word
to the aints so that they will become the saints. Again, I say "That the
minister delivers the word to the aints, so they will become the saints."

He or she brings the word to all the Saints and the Aints. They
minister to get the spirit and the soul to be straight, not to be
bent over or crippled, but standing tall, but wait that is not all.
They help to repair and restore all men, to teach them not to bow to sin.

Ministry is what we must do, to compel the gospel
so people can become free, and delivered
totally, to have a renewed mind and an increase in
faith, to provide hope to stay in the race.
Ministry is what we should do, to spread the
gospel around the world. To inform every
woman, man boy, and girl. So this is a call to welcome
you in, to welcome you in before the end.
Repent; be baptized so that you can live free, and to live eternally.
It is all about Ministry. So read your word, and
you will see that Jesus died so that you
can be free!
Ministry Is:

    M=Moving
    I= In
    N=Newness
    I=Inspired
    S=Strength
    T=Transcending
    R=Revived Revelation
    Y=Yoked up with Jesus Christ
Ministry – It is what we all should do.

EMBRACE
(Dedicated to my friends and Pastor Tony Sellers and Evangelist Cynthia Sellers)

Embrace: means to include encircle, to clasp in the arms, cherish, love,
embrace your sisters and your brothers,
embrace not only black and white, but
embrace every race,
embrace the Asians, Mexicans, Indians, Africans, Caucasian,
bi-racial, and the Chinese just to name a few.
Embrace every nationality,
embrace is not just for the democrat or republican,
embrace is not only for the rich, but
embracing includes the middle class, as well as the poor,
embrace across the nation;
embrace our presidents, governors, mayors, Pastors and senators too,
embrace across the land.
Embrace in Texas, North Dakota, and Ohio, embrace in upper
class neighborhoods and well as the lower class neighborhoods.
Embrace in Egypt, Scotland, Pakistan, Russia and Jamaica
and this is only naming a few. Embrace across the land.
Embrace the alcoholics, the individuals on drugs,
the homosexuals, and the homeless.
embrace the Methodist, Catholic, Apostolic, Pentecostal, Jehovah
Witness, Greek, Jew and Gentile, again embrace, embrace,
embrace every race. God says "welcome all", he did not say
all would make it into heaven, but to embrace with love.
Embrace on the golf course or at putt-putt;
embrace on the ocean or on the lake,
embrace the Millionaire or the minimum wage employee.
Embrace the educated professor with a PHD, but
also embrace the individual with a GED.
It's all about love and diversity.
Embrace in the Public Schools, Christian Schools, Sunday schools,
and also pre-schools.
Embrace in the White House, the Black House,
The Court House, your house, my house and in

Gods' House.
Embrace with love all across the land,
Embrace your Heritage, and embrace in this land,
embrace every race and allow love to spread.

CHOSEN

Out of all the men and women,
from all the ships in the sea,
God has reached, selected, called and chosen me,
to step out of darkness, and to follow after him,
He has placed his trust and abides in me,
to carry the word, and deliver it to thee,
to compel whatever he speaks, yes
he has chosen me.
He has called me to lead, to lead the people in need,
to show them the way out of bondage and defeat.
He has chosen me through
His precious blood and authority,
called, selected and chosen by he,
The Lord, Jehovah, Jesus
called me.

WAVES OF THE SEA

Waves of the Sea,
come from me, the great majesty,
the wind, the rain,
because I reign, the great I Am,
the ocean is full, but never over-flowing, and
I am the well that never runs dry,
the waves of the deep blue sea says, "Come"
follow after me", but you ask where will
It carry me?
Jesus is the captain on board of this ship,
on the sea can you trust him to navigate thee?
Jesus says "come, follow after me,
we can sail together for eternity.

GOD LOOKS AT THE HEART
(to Prophetess Melva Perry, and Pastor Eddie Perry of Heart of a Woman Ministries and Love Ministries)]

When you by pass the surface, the outer core,
the shell, the flesh, the skin,
What do you see?
Yes, the heart, the core, the rhythm, the beat,
the drum, the hymn, the most essential,
and central part, called the heart.

Out of the heart, flows the issues of life and the mouth speaks.

Is your life worth living, is your heart worth beating,
repetitiously, fast or slow with a pace maker or on its
own. It is the heart that makes things start.
It pumps the blood, it causes things to flow,
and it creates life, so you can go.

The heart gets weak, the heart gets strong,
the heart is tender, and can cause
one to surrender.
God allows the heart to heal, he mends, he
strengthens, he revives, he resuscitates,
God looks pass your past, he sees your future,
he gives new starts, and he gives new
hearts, God looks at the heart.

FIRE!

Fire, Fire,
My desire is release of the fire of the Holy Ghost,
Fire, fire,
allow this fire to fall on those from the gutter,
to the upper most.
Fire, fire,
allow this fire to fall, to spread, and all
women, and men to be lead,
allow this fire
to purge, to cleanse, to blow away the ashes of sin,
and to allow life to begin again,
Fire, fire, Holy Ghost fire
fall, spread and allow, children, women and
men to be lead.

VIEW THE WORLD

Get out and see the world, there is so much to do,
Just do not become a fool, and try to avoid hooking
up with the wrong crew,
get out and view the scenes, just remember
that everything is not always green,
the world is a big place; there are lots of lanes,
a lot of lights, also a lot of fortune and fame,
there is a wide road, and a narrow road,
but always remember it is up to you as to which
road you will choose.

SET APART

Set apart, set apart,
first, set apart in the heart,
set apart so that you may start to heal a people,
and to heal the land. Set apart to do a work that
is designed with the masters hand,
set apart to touch a certain mass of people in the nation,
so that others can become free, but first, set apart
in the heart.

I JUST CALLED

I just called to spread a little cheer,
to let you know that Jesus is near,
not to fear, but to adhere, and really
recognize that Jesus is real. He lives,
he dwells, he reigns, and rules,
The Lord is here

RAINBOW

Rainbow up in the sky,
see it as you're passing by,
rainbow standing out
to let the world know
what it is all about,
the colors in the bow,
will let you know,
the flood is over, and
will come no more.

HAVE FUN

Have fun, and enjoy life,
get away from misery and strife,
Have fun, enjoy life.
smile a while, laugh a lot,
take a day, go to a play, go to the mall,
go for a swim, go to the zoo, or spend
the day with your friend,
go for a run, just have fun.

TEENS DON'T BE MEAN

Teens, don't be mean, rejoice, get up and sing, teens don't be mean,
so what, everyone is trying to be cool, you just remain in school.
Keep your virginity, because it is your identity.
You do not have to be lame or be part of any gang, be yourself.
Teens, don't be mean.
Remove any anger, and rejection,
don't allow it to be a part of your reflection.
dark side, you must go, because this young girl will not be your
property, and go to the wrong places that you decided to go.

Teens do not be mean, don't get laid to get paid, or possibly
contact a STD. don't be a part of any type of corrupt crowd,
stand out and be proud. So they talk about you, then let them
talk, because when it comes to graduation time, you will walk.
Teens, don't be mean. Remember, juvenile delinquency
is a sting, and it sometimes results from being mean,
so don't be mean, but enjoy and just be a teen.

LITTLE CHILDREN LET ME IN

Little children, little children, let me in. Let me in so that you will not sin. Learn of me, while you are young so that you will not become dumb. Yes, your education is great, but I'm even greater than your degree. You see, without me giving you knowledge, health, and strength, You would be nothing. So, you see, you need me. Little children, little children let me in. I am wisdom, and want to impart into you.

CHILDREN WANT TO HAVE FUN

Children just want to have fun,
children want to rip and run.
they need room to play,
they need to be corrected of their mistakes,
they look to adults, and want their superiors to
show them the way, but yet, they want to have fun
and play in the sun. Children just want to have fun.

SECOND WIND

When you open, breathe in; get rid of your sins,
repent so that your healing will begin, and you will
grasp your second wind.
Second wind, second wind,
I welcome the second wind to enter in,
sitting by the seashore, or by an open door,
breathe in and receive your second wind.

BREATHE ON ME

Breathe on me, so I can be complete in thee,
breathe on me, so I can see the things you have
purposely desired of me,
breathe on me, so I can receive everything that is
meant for me.
Breathe on me; breathe your life directly into me,
so, I can be liberated, transformed and made free.
breathe on me.

I MUST FLY HIGH

I must fly and excel high,
I must reach my goals, and
achieve my dreams, so therefore,
I must fly high,
I must fly high,
I must fly like the eagle in the sky,
soaring with wide open wings,
I must fly high,
I must fly high above the highest mountains,
way up on the top,
I must go higher, and higher, and soar
with the Messiah, I must fly high.

PRAISE AND LIFT HIM HIGH

Elohim El Shadi,
praise and lift him high,
praise him early,
praise him late,
praise him while you wait,
Elohim, El Shadi,
praise, praise is what you do,
praise him on the mountains,
praise in the valley low,
praise him wherever you may go,
Elohim, El-Shadi,
praise and lift him high.

WE MUST STAND

We must stand,
shootings, and stabbings everywhere,
violence and dead spirits fill the air,
strong holds, darkness everywhere,
sneaking, peeping, and lots of creeping
all across the land come on Christians,
we must stand.
Allow your light to shine in these last
and trying times,
murders, rapes, and lions on escape,
drugs, sex, alcohol, Christian, saints of God,
we must stand tall.
AIDS, and divorce sweeping the land,
women, men, and children of God,
we must stand.

SHINE YOUR LIGHT

Shine your light from your light house, because Gods light will shine
from his light house. Let God's light shine through thee,
"pick up your cross, and follow after me," says the Lord,
It's at the cross where I shed my blood at Calvary,
It's at the cross where I shed my blood for thee.
Pick up yourself, shake yourself off, lift yourself up, and look up,
set yourself free, let my light shine through thee, and continue
to follow after me

ONE NIGHT WITH THE KING OF KINGS

One night with The King of Kings, changes everything;
It can change your mind; it can change your circumstances,
It can change your environment; it can change your Income status,
One night with The King of Kings, It can change your anointing,
It can change how you pray, it can change when you pray, and
it can change your vision, it can change your perception.
One night with The Kings of Kings,
can change your living arrangement;
It can change your appearance,
and or your attitude; it can even change your Name,
It can change your marital status, yes, one night with the King
of Kings, can make a significant difference in your life.
One night can cause you to forgive, and allow
you to live healthier, and happier,
One night, one night, one night with The King of Kings changes
everything, but to get in the presence of this King, requires some
things, you see with this King, you can't manipulate, you can't
fake him out, you can't win him over with a phony smile or with a
twitch, or switch; you can't sip and dip with The King of Kings,
One night, one night, one night with The King of Kings.

FLOWER

A woman is like a flower; she can be so free, full of life,
and without any disease. Sometimes, a flower needs to be
pruned, shaped, molded, fed, and reserved. Women are like
flowers. There are such a variety of flowers, different sizes,
shapes, colors, scents, and roots, just like a woman.
Plant a seed and watch a flower grow; it buds, and then
blossoms, just as the women of today, and women of
yesterday. It can grow on a single stem or within a group.
A flower can produce year after year with Mother Nature's care.
Just like flowers need sunshine, they also need the rain, just like
our lives, we sometimes have sunshine, and some days there
is pain, but if we hold up, we won't wither away, flowers are
unique, it can be a rose, a daffodil, iris, begonia, or daisy, they
are all similar in some type of way, so be like a flower that is free,
and full of life, like a woman who blossoms in Jesus Christ.

DON'T LOOK BACK

Don't look back, don't look back,
If you look back, you may get off track,
Keep moving forward, and allow your feet
to be ordered, you must release yourself from
your past, and press towards the mark of the
prize of the high calling, don't look back,
Do you remember the pillar of salt?
Oh, but it was it her fault, she looked back,
don't look back.

RACE

Does your race identify the place where you stand in life?
Does your race determine who you are, and where your destiny is?
Does the color of your face, say you are not a part of the human race?
Does your race determine your place, your residence or your school?
Where you shop or where your dine, is it your race or the color
of your face?

PAIN

Pain, pain,
you do not know the pain
that almost made me insane,
and, don't begin to place any blame,
because your situation may have created
some shame. You do not know the pain,
yes, the hurt was or is still deep, but
you yet have the opportunity to reach the
mountain peak. The stain of the pain does
not have to remain

ANGER

Anger, anger, go away,
why does this anger want to stay?
"Move," I said, anger go away,
I don't have time today for this type
of anger to attach and stay, so
anger, anger go away.

SOMETIMES YOU MAY GET LOW

Sometimes, you may get low,
so you will know what it is like to be on the bottom,
sometimes, while in your low state,
you will really learn how to appreciate,
sometimes, it may seem as though you can't get up,
it may seem like you're stuck;
just don't give up.
Sometimes, when you are low, you don't know which way to go,
sometimes, while you are low,
you will overcome hurdles you didn't know,
These things come to help you to grow, so the next time you get low,
Just do not give up and let go.

ARE YOU STRAPPED

Are you strapped, caught in a trap,
going through a maze, a phase, or
simply in a daze? Stretch your arms towards
heaven and call on the name of Jesus to lift you
from the snare, to remove the glare, to remove
the trap, the strap, or the zap.

WHERE IS YOUR SOUL

Is the soul a deep black hole, or is it something that makes one whole?
Is the soul something that we can't explain, but yet, feel the pain?
Is the soul like soul food with many flavors,
or is the soul hollow, seeking something or someone to follow?
Does the soul stand alone, and operate on its own?
Is the soul connected to the body or to the heart?
Does the soul weep, does the soul sleep, or does the soul speak?
Where is your soul, and who is it connected to?
Is your soul lost or is it found?
Is it stable, solid or on the ground?
Where is your soul?

GOD ALREADY KNOWS

In times of fear, in times of cheer, God already knows,
you are being tested, you are being tried to see what you
will decide. God already knows,
will you run, or will you hide, or will you allow
God to decide?

JESUS ALL THE WAY
(to the tune of jingle bells)

Jesus Christ, Jesus Christ,
Jesus all the way,
oh, what fun it is to know
Jesus all the way!

Jesus Christ, Jesus Christ,
Jesus all the way,
oh, what fun it is to know
Jesus all the way!

As we travel through the snow,
and climb over all the hills,
He's the one who makes the way
each and every day,

Jesus Christ, Jesus Christ,
Jesus all the way,
oh, what fun it is to know
Jesus all the way
Hey!

WOMEN BE STRONG

Women be strong – continue to hold onto God's unchanging hand,
women hold on. Don't go for anyone's husband, wait for your own,
women, hold out, women be strong.

Single women, married women, widowed women, young women,
be strong, I encourage you to hold on.

Don't fall prey to the adversary's wicked devices of this lustful world,
it can look glamourous, and beautiful, but don't allow it to fool you.
Temptation is everywhere on every side, so you must be strong.

You sometimes get weary, tired, and even weak, but
that does not mean defeat. You sometimes just want
to give in, but hold on, be strong and resist sin.

You don't want to hear the word, pray, fast or read the word, realize by
not doing these things can create an open door. Women be strong.

Yes, we have all been hurt, used, rejected, or mistreated in some
kind of way, but don't allow it to be an excuse to live any type of
way. Be strong and hold on, your time, and season will come.

You don't have to date everybody you meet, and don't
give up your body to just anybody on the street. Hold
on; keep yourself for our real mate, your true date.
Single women, married women, widowed women, young women,
be strong, and hold onto God's unfailing love. Women be strong.

EVERYTHING COMING AT ME

Everything is coming at me- mortgage past due,
my daughter is late for school,
my brother just went to jail,
and grandma is telling everybody to go to hell.
The boss just received word to discharge you,
and turn around and take the company to the zoo,
your baby was just diagnosed with the flu,
and all your bills are late too.
You scream, "what should I do? Everything is coming at me!"

I am going blind, and now, I can hardly see, I scream,
I shout, and pout saying "everything is coming at me,"
and I hear the enemy laughing, "Ha, ha, ha!"
Yet, I rise, and when everything is coming at me,
I fall down on my knees, that is where I get the victory.

WHEN WE DON'T KNOW

At times, we don't know how life is going to turn,
at times, we do not know
If our decisions are wrong or right.
At times, life brings one to the a stage of the unknown.
You ask yourself the question, do I continue, do I stand still,
should I ask for help, or do things on my own?
Step back, lay low, pray and take it slow,
and remember that whatever happens, God already knows.

END OF THE ROPE

Are you at the end of your rope, and lost your hope, so you turn to dope, tired, fed up, and can't seem to get ahead, you find yourself in somebody's bed, all your bills are overdue, and you do not know what to do, so you drown your sorrows in a bottle. Are you at the end of your rope, and just can't cope, there is another way, through The Word of God, try God for your dope, for your bed of comfort, there is life in The Word. (The Holy Bible), so you say, "I tried God before," well, it's time to go to God again, don't try God, just repent, and be determined that this time you will win, be a defeater, and victorious. There is no failure in God. He Is your hope at the end of the rope.

BREAK THE CURSE

Break the curse, break the cycle, the back, and forth, the in and out, the up, and down, the around, and around. Break the curse, break the cycle, of lack, and poverty, break the curse, break the cycle of fornication, and adultery, break the curse, break the cycle of (GGG) gambling, gluttony, and gin, break the curse, break the cycle of pornography, lust, and no trust, break the curse, break the cycles.

WOMEN

Women are special, and uniquely designed, women are one
of a kind, women have power, potential, and self-will. Women
are special. Married, single, widowed, or divorced, young, old,
rich or poor, mother or non-mother you have a purpose.

Women you need to encourage one another, and sometimes you have
to encourage yourself. To the single women don't be down in despair,
lift your head, and know that God is near. Married women – don't get
depressed, know that the Lord knows your test, and in God, there is
rest. Childless women – don't think of yourself as less, but know that
you are blessed. Widowed women – have no fears, God will supply
your need. Divorced or separated, be encouraged, life does go on, and
to the mother with many demands, lean to God's unchanging hand.

Women are special and all have a place, but you must continue to
run the race. No matter what circumstances or situations that may
come your way, you just know that you can pray. Older women are to
teach the younger women, so we all have a job to do, so be obedient,
and keep trusting the Lord. Jesus is a keeper; sustainer, maintainer,
provider, and he will never leave you or forsake you, so do his will.

MEN

Men are unique and strong creatures too!
They also have responsibilities, and jobs to do,
real men are not wimps, nor are they pimps.
They will work, and receive an honest living.
They will provide and not hide.
They respect the woman who gave birth,
who brought forth a child to dwell on the earth.
They may produce the seed, but it is the woman who bleeds.
She is designed to nurture, and to help supply the needs).
Every father is not a dad, so don't get mad,
every man is not a father,
and that does not make him any less,
so we pray that all the men are blessed.

FRESH NEW START

My mind was just about blown to bits, I was almost about to call it quits, that is when Jesus stepped in on the scene, removed my sins, and made me whole again. I'm talking about the blood, the blood of Jesus. It forgives us of our sins, and makes one whole again.

I don't need any crack, or cocaine, any alcohol or nicotine; that is because of the blood, the blood of Jesus, replaces those things. I don't have to lust, worry, or fret, because Jesus died upon the cross. I'm talking about the blood, the blood of Jesus. We all make mistakes, and fall short. The word says, we all have sinned and come short of the glory of God, but because of mercy and because of grace, we can continue to seek God's face.

We can get back up and move forward again. I'm talking about the blood, the blood of Jesus; it removes all sins, and makes us whole again. But you must repent, and be baptized, and allow Jesus to enter inside. Confess with your mouth, and believe in your heart, and Jesus Christ will give you a fresh, new start.

NEW DAY!

It's a new day!
try a new way,
begin by starting to pray,
ask for a new start,
ask for a new heart,
It's a new day,
see the sunrise,
watch the sunset,
feel the ocean breeze,
relax under a shade tree,
It's a new day!
praise God,
Hooray!

Isaiah (KJV) 43:19
Behold, I will do a new thing;

ABOUT THE AUTHOR

 Sherry Leonard of Columbus Ohio, a Disciple of Christ, Mother of three wonderful adult children Shaniece, Michele and Randolph, a lovely daughter-in-law Ashley, three beautiful granddaughters Jaylynn, Kiarrah, and Lamaiah, I'm an employee in the State of Ohio, a student at Columbus State Community College, an Inspirational writer; evangelist, member of Higher Dimensions Ministries. and the recent branching out and birthing of Eagle Christian Fellowship

For Conferences, events, preaching, teaching or poetry
Write: Sherry Leonard
P.O. Box 604
Brice, OH 43109
Neicytx4@yahoo.com
EAGLE CHRISTIAN FELLOWSHIP

Printed in the United States
By Bookmasters